I0185383

STUDY GUIDE

# Death.by
# *Pastoring*

Copyright © 2024 by Shane and Sue Schlesman

Published by AVAIL

All rights reserved. No portion of this book may be reproduced, stored in a retrieval system, or transmitted in any form or by any means—electronic, mechanical, photocopy, recording, scanning, or other—except for brief quotations in critical reviews or articles, without prior written permission of the author.

Unless otherwise noted, scripture quotations are taken from the Holy Bible, New International Version®, NIV®. Copyright © 1973, 1978, 1984, 2011 by Biblica, Inc.™ Used by permission of Zondervan. All rights reserved worldwide. www.zondervan.com. The "NIV" and "New International Version" are trademarks registered in the United States Patent and Trademark Office by Biblica, Inc.™ | Scripture quotations marked KJV are taken from the King James Version of the Bible. Public domain. | Scripture quotations marked MSG are taken from THE MESSAGE, copyright © 1993, 1994, 1995, 1996, 2000, 2001, 2002 by Eugene H. Peterson. Used by permission of NavPress. All rights reserved. Represented by Tyndale House Publishers, Inc. | Scripture quotations marked NLT are taken from the Holy Bible, New Living Translation, copyright © 1996, 2004, 2015 by Tyndale House Foundation. Used by permission of Tyndale House Publishers, Inc., Carol Stream, Illinois 60188. All rights reserved. | Scripture quotations marked TLB are taken from The Living Bible copyright © 1971 by Tyndale House Foundation. Used by permission of Tyndale House Publishers Inc., Carol Stream, Illinois 60188. All rights reserved. The Living Bible, TLB, and The Living Bible logo are registered trademarks of Tyndale House Publishers.

For foreign and subsidiary rights, contact the author.

Cover design by Sara Young
Cover photo by Andrew van Tilborgh

ISBN: 978-1-960678-18-8      1  2  3  4  5  6  7  8  9  10

*Printed in the United States of America*

STUDY GUIDE

# Death.by
# Pastoring

*Finding the Heartbeat of a Healthy Leader*

## Shane and Sue Schlesman

AVAIL

# CONTENTS

**PART 1. THE SILENT KILLER (THE PROBLEM OF STRESS)**........................7

Chapter 1. The Almost-Death of a Pastor (and His Wife) ....................................................8

Chapter 2. The DNA of Stress.................................... 14

Chapter 3. What We Didn't Learn in Seminary .............. 20

Chapter 4. The Snare of Expectation ......................... 26

Chapter 5. A Bottomless Pit....................................... 32

**PART 2. A NEW WAY TO WORK (THE HOPE FOR STRESS)**..................... 37

Chapter 6. A Message for the Heavy-Hearted................. 38

Chapter 7. The Pathway to Peace ................................ 44

Chapter 8. Leading in a Yoke..................................... 50

Chapter 9. Stewards and Owners................................ 56

Chapter 10. A Lighter Load........................................ 62

**PART 3. A NEW WAY TO REST (THE REDEMPTION OF STRESS)**............. 69

Chapter 11. The Good Shepherd.................................. 70

Chapter 12. Rest Versus Restoration .......................... 76

Chapter 13. New Walk, Same Valley ........................... 82

Chapter 14. A Seat at the Table ................................. 88

Chapter 15. In My Father's House .............................. 94

# Death.by Pastoring

*Finding the Heartbeat of a Healthy Leader*

Shane and Sue
Schlesman

# PART ONE

# THE SILENT KILLER (THE PROBLEM OF STRESS)

CHAPTER 1

# THE ALMOST-DEATH OF A PASTOR (AND HIS WIFE)

*We never think our stress is as dangerous as it actually is.*

## READING TIME

As you read Chapter 1: "The Almost-Death of a Pastor (and His Wife)" in *Death by Pastoring*, review, reflect on, and respond to the text by answering the following questions.

# REVIEW, REFLECT, AND RESPOND:

Reflect on Shane's initial response to the physical symptoms during the bike ride. How might his perception of personal health and stress align with common misconceptions, and what lessons can be drawn from his experience? What is your own perception of personal health and stress?

_____

_____

_____

_____

_____

_____

_____

_____

_____

_____

_____

_____

_____

_____

_____

_____

_____

_____

_____

_____

_____

Consider the factors influencing Shane's reluctance to acknowledge the possibility of a heart attack. How might his attitude be reflective of broader societal attitudes towards health, and what insights can be gained from this? Have you or someone close to you ever responded to health in a similar manner? Describe the experience.

_____

_____

_____

_____

_____

_____

_____

_____

_____

Explore Sue's actions and approach in convincing Shane to seek medical attention. In what ways did her response showcase qualities of care and concern, and how can you apply similar approaches in your own relationships?

_____

_____

_____

_____

_____

_____

_____

_____

_____

_____

Examine the role played by Shane's son Brent, a physical therapist, in recognizing the severity of the situation. How can one's professional background influence their ability to perceive and respond to health-related issues within their family? Have you ever experienced this?

_____

_____

_____

_____

_____

_____

_____

_____

_____

Reflect on how Shane and Sue's experience with the heart attack prompted them to reevaluate their understanding of stress. How can individuals apply the lessons learned to reassess their own approach to stress management, particularly in the context of their personal and professional lives? Practically, what does this look like for you?

_____

_____

_____

_____

_____

_____

_____

_____

_____

> *"Anyone who loves their father or mother more than me is not worthy of me; anyone who loves their son or daughter more than me is not worthy of me."*
>
> —**Matthew 10:37 (NIV)**

*Consider the scripture above and answer the following questions:*

What is the meaning of this verse?

_____

_____

_____

_____

_____

_____

_____

_____

_____

What would it look like if you fully applied this verse to your life?

_____

_____

_____

_____

_____

_____

_____

_____

# HEALTHY HEARTBEATS FOR
## The Almost-Death of a Pastor (and His Wife)

1) Write down the most stressful situations you've been through in the last five years. How have you processed the stress? Who helped you? Run the list by someone who knows you well and get their feedback on the stress you experienced during these times and how you handled it.

_____

_____

_____

_____

_____

_____

_____

_____

2) Take the "Stress Assessment" in the Resources at the back of the book.

3) Read *Zeal Without Burnout* by Christopher Ash and *The Resilient Pastor* by Glenn Packiam.

# THE DNA OF STRESS

*Stress is God's natural switch for biological function, the breaker in our body's breaker box that flips whenever we overload the circuits.*

## READING TIME

As you read Chapter 2: "The DNA of Stress" in *Death by Pastoring*, review, reflect on, and respond to the text by answering the following questions.

# REVIEW, REFLECT, AND RESPOND:

Reflect on Sue's struggle with meeting the book deadline and the stress it brought. How does her reaction to this situation reveal common misconceptions about handling stress? Have you ever reacted in this way in a similar situation? Consider how societal expectations play a role in exacerbating stress for high-achieving individuals.

_____

_____

_____

_____

_____

_____

_____

_____

_____

_____

_____

_____

_____

_____

_____

_____

_____

_____

_____

_____

_____

Explore Sue's realization about her own anxiety and the difficulty she faced articulating it. How can the stigma around mental health issues, even within oneself, hinder the ability to address and manage stress effectively? Have you ever failed to confront your anxiety or stress due to mental health stigma? Describe the experience, and discuss the importance of self-awareness in stress management.

_____

_____

_____

_____

_____

_____

_____

_____

Delve into the impact of Shane's heart attack on Sue's stress levels. How did the fear of another heart attack influence her daily activities, particularly in terms of shopping, food preparation, and managing the responsibilities of ministry? Has your life been negatively affected by your fear of something out of your control? What were the effects? Consider the interconnectedness of stress, trauma, and the body's response.

_____

_____

_____

_____

_____

_____

_____

How do individual personalities and coping strategies manifest in high-stress situations, and what insights can be gained from recognizing and adjusting these patterns? What personalities and coping strategies do you manifest in the presence of stress? Are these negative? Explain.

_____

_____

_____

_____

_____

_____

_____

_____

_____

Investigate the concept of stress as a natural biological response, as explained by Jeff Bezos. How does stress, when left unmanaged, affect the body's biology and lead to long-term consequences? Discuss the importance of recognizing and addressing stress signals to maintain overall well-being.

_____

_____

_____

_____

_____

_____

_____

_____

_____

Can you relate to Shane's practices to prioritize self-care in the midst of a demanding work schedule? Discuss the role of your self-awareness in preventing stress-related health issues.

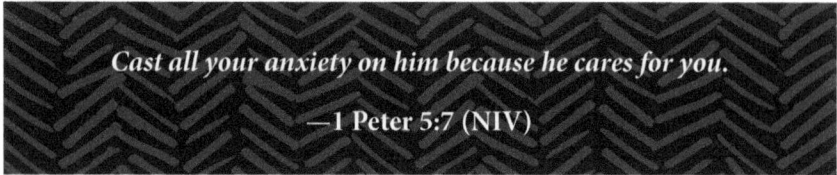

_____

_____

_____

_____

_____

_____

_____

_____

_____

_____

*Cast all your anxiety on him because he cares for you.*

**—1 Peter 5:7 (NIV)**

*Consider the scripture above and answer the following question:*

What does it mean to "cast your anxiety" on God?

_____

_____

_____

_____

_____

_____

_____

_____

# HEALTHY HEARTBEATS FOR
## The DNA of Stress

1) Ask yourself: What causes your heart rate to go up? What situations or people make you panic? Get help to eliminate, delegate, or get assistance.

_____

_____

_____

_____

_____

_____

2) Read *The Self-Aware Leader* by John Maxwell.

3) Slowly read and process the research and therapies in *The Body Keeps the Score* by Bessel Van Der Kolk, M.D.

4) Consider buying an Oura ring and monitoring your HRV.

5) Practice yoga, stretching, spiritual meditation, and deep breathing. These practices calm down your parasympathetic nervous system.

6) Look at your schedule. Limit the amount of adversarial or stressful meetings you have each day and each week. Choose the minimum that you can emotionally handle and stick to your limit.

# WHAT WE DIDN'T LEARN IN SEMINARY

*We weren't ready for the load of
carrying people's burdens and the
attached spiritual weight.*

As you read Chapter 3: "What We Didn't Learn in Seminary" in *Death by Pastoring*, review, reflect on, and respond to the text by answering the following questions.

# REVIEW, REFLECT, AND RESPOND:

What challenges does this chapter mention that weren't adequately addressed in their seminary training? When have you been faced with unseen challenges, and how did you respond?

_____
_____
_____
_____
_____
_____
_____
_____
_____
_____
_____
_____
_____
_____
_____
_____
_____
_____
_____
_____
_____

According to this chapter, what are some statistics and challenges that pastors and their spouses experience in ministry? Have you experienced any of these?

_____

_____

_____

_____

_____

_____

_____

_____

_____

_____

In what ways does the analogy of training for a race relate to the challenges of pastoral leadership and the mental game involved?

_____

_____

_____

_____

_____

_____

_____

_____

_____

_____

_____

What insights does this chapter provide regarding the intersection of pain, faith, and ministry, especially in terms of handling suffering?

_____

_____

_____

_____

_____

_____

_____

_____

_____

_____

_____

How does this chapter describe the idea of leaving one's current ministry and the potential challenges and consequences associated with such a decision?

_____

_____

_____

_____

_____

_____

_____

_____

_____

_____

_____

How does pastoral leadership stress differ from stress in other professions, and what unique aspects contribute to the challenges faced by pastors?

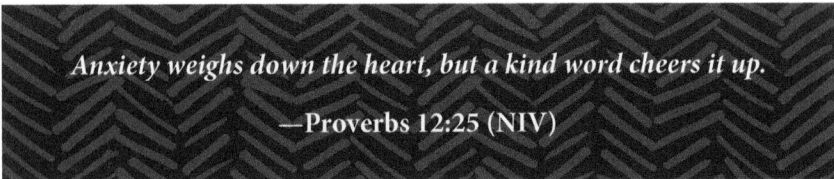

_____

_____

_____

_____

_____

_____

_____

_____

_____

*Anxiety weighs down the heart, but a kind word cheers it up.*

**—Proverbs 12:25 (NIV)**

*Consider the scripture above and answer the following question:*

Have you ever experienced a kind word that helped quell your anxiety? Describe the situation.

_____

_____

_____

_____

_____

_____

_____

_____

_____

# HEALTHY HEARTBEATS FOR
## What We Didn't Learn in Seminary

1) Whether or not you attended seminary, what preconceived ideas did you have about pastoring before you became a pastor? How have you processed the reality of pastoring?

_____

_____

_____

_____

_____

_____

_____

2) Find a Christian counselor. To help facilitate vulnerability and safety, we recommend telehealth or finding counselors who aren't familiar with your church. You need to be able to speak freely.

3) Read *The 21 Irrefutable Laws of Leadership* by John Maxwell and *A Glorious Dark* by A. J. Swoboda.

# THE SNARE OF EXPECTATION

*Share your stress with a wise person who can give you perspective. Learn to delegate.*

## READING TIME

As you read Chapter 4: "The Snare of Expectation" in *Death by Pastoring*, review, reflect on, and respond to the text by answering the following questions.

# REVIEW, REFLECT, AND RESPOND:

What impact do unrealistic expectations have on individuals, particularly in the context of leadership and ministry?

_____

_____

_____

_____

_____

_____

_____

_____

_____

_____

_____

_____

_____

_____

_____

_____

_____

_____

_____

_____

_____

_____

_____

This chapter mentions three biblical figures—David, Moses, and Elijah—and their approaches to handling expectations. How does each leader deal with expectations, and what lessons can be drawn from their experiences?

_____

_____

_____

_____

_____

_____

_____

_____

_____

_____

_____

Describe the unbiblical nature of expectations and how they can be detrimental to individuals.

_____

_____

_____

_____

_____

_____

_____

_____

_____

_____

What role do values play in managing stress and expectations? How can leaders use their values to navigate challenges and prevent misaligned expectations?

_____

_____

_____

_____

_____

_____

_____

_____

_____

_____

_____

The warning of expectation section highlights potential stressors created by others' expectations. How can you deal with stressors related to process, personality, and responsibility in a ministry context?

_____

_____

_____

_____

_____

_____

_____

_____

_____

_____

_____

*As the deer pants for streams of water, so my soul pants for you, my God. My soul thirsts for God, for the living God. When can I go and meet with God? My tears have been my food day and night, while people say to me all day long, "Where is your God?" These things I remember as I pour out my soul: how I used to go to the house of God under the protection of the Mighty One with shouts of joy and praise among the festive throng.*

—Psalm 42:1-5 (NIV)

*Consider the scripture above and answer the following questions:*

What stands out to you from this passage?

_____

_____

_____

_____

_____

_____

_____

_____

How can you apply this passage to your life?

_____

_____

_____

_____

_____

_____

_____

_____

# HEALTHY HEARTBEATS FOR
## The Snare of Expectation

1) What tasks that you currently manage do you have to do? If you ignore tradition and expectation, which responsibilities should you delegate?

_____

_____

_____

_____

_____

_____

2) Identify your top three spiritual gifts. How do you activate these for the benefit of the body? Now, set up a plan for off-loading everything else.

_____

_____

_____

_____

_____

3) Read *Resilient* by John Eldredge and subscribe to his "Pause" App. Do the mental and physical breathing exercises.

4) Read *The Gifts of Imperfection* or *Atlas of the Heart* by Brené Brown. While not Christian books, you will be astounded at the spiritual applications you can make as you read them.

5) What difficult decisions are you currently making? Identify the core value that feeds your fear. Meditate on God's truth and adjust your values, if necessary.

# A BOTTOMLESS PIT

*Grief is grief.*

## READING TIME

As you read Chapter 5: "A Bottomless Pit" in *Death by Pastoring*, review, reflect on, and respond to the text by answering the following questions.

# REVIEW, REFLECT, AND RESPOND:

In your own words, what is the difference between anxiety and worry? How do they operate in the brain?

_____

_____

_____

_____

_____

_____

_____

_____

_____

_____

_____

_____

_____

_____

_____

_____

_____

_____

_____

_____

_____

_____

_____

What tools does God provide to help individuals avoid, conquer, and redeem anxiety?

_____

_____

_____

_____

_____

_____

_____

_____

_____

_____

In what way does Peter address anxiety and provide directives for overcoming it?

_____

_____

_____

_____

_____

_____

_____

_____

_____

_____

What is the significance of the lion metaphor in relation to the devil's actions, and how does this chapter suggest resisting the devil's attacks?

_____

_____

_____

_____

_____

_____

_____

_____

_____

_____

How does grief manifest, and what is the role of faith in navigating through grief?

_____

_____

_____

_____

_____

_____

_____

_____

_____

_____

_____

> *Roaring lions that tear their prey open their mouths wide against me. I am poured out like water, and all my bones are out of joint. My heart has turned to wax; it has melted within me. My mouth has dried up like a potsherd, and my tongue sticks to the roof of my mouth; you lay me in the dust of death.*
>
> **—Psalm 22:13-15 (NIV)**

*Consider the scripture above and answer the following question:*

What do you feel is the meaning of this psalm?

_____

_____

_____

_____

## HEALTHY HEARTBEATS:
### A Bottomless Pit

1) Read *On Grief and Grieving* by David Kessler and Elisabeth Kubler-Ross, *Forgiving What You Can't Forget* by Lysa TerKeurst, and/or *Get Out of That Pit* by Beth Moore.

2) See a grief therapist. Look into EMDR, a therapy developed for overriding your sympathetic nervous system so you can process your loss and implement recovery.

3) Start a thankfulness journal. Every day, write down at least three things you're thankful for in a journal or in your phone notes.

4) Listen to the Brittany Jones interview on Stress Test Podcast, "Break the Stigma: A Pastor's Journey with Mental Health," Episode 11, 21 Sept. 2023.

# PART TWO

# A NEW WAY TO WORK (THE HOPE FOR STRESS)

# A MESSAGE FOR THE HEAVY-HEARTED

*Only when Jesus operates as the authority
of our lives can he give us rest.*

## READING TIME

As you read Chapter 6: "A Message for the Heavy-Hearted" in *Death by Pastoring*, review, reflect on, and respond to the text by answering the following questions.

# REVIEW, REFLECT, AND RESPOND:

How would you describe the early days of your pastoral ministry, as well as the emotions associated with it?

_____

_____

_____

_____

_____

_____

_____

_____

_____

_____

_____

_____

_____

_____

_____

_____

_____

_____

_____

_____

_____

According to this chapter, why do ministry expectations often lead to disappointment? Have you ever experienced disappointment from your ministry expectations?

_____

_____

_____

_____

_____

_____

_____

_____

_____

_____

In what ways can it be argued that Jesus was not a workaholic? How did Jesus approach his work, and how can pastors learn from it?

_____

_____

_____

_____

_____

_____

_____

_____

_____

_____

_____

What is the significance of the term "anapaou" (rest) in Matthew 11:28, and how does Jesus promise to provide rest in the context of work?

_____

_____

_____

_____

_____

_____

_____

_____

_____

_____

How should ministers approach rest, and what is the connection between rest and the quality of work?

_____

_____

_____

_____

_____

_____

_____

_____

_____

_____

Which forms of resting are mentioned in this chapter, and which of these can you apply in your life?

_____

_____

_____

_____

_____

_____

_____

_____

_____

_____

_____

*"Come to me, all you who are weary and burdened, and I will give you rest."*

**—Matthew 11:28 (NIV)**

*Consider the scripture above and answer the following question:*

What kind of weariness is Jesus Christ talking about in this verse?

_____

_____

_____

_____

_____

_____

_____

# HEALTHY HEARTBEATS FOR
## A Message for the Heavy-Hearted

1) Listen to Scott Wilson's interview called "Embracing Sabbatical" on *Stress Test Podcast*, Episode 6, and Mark Batterson's interview called "Three Powerful Words to Lower Your Stress" on *Stress Test Podcast*, Episode 4, June 12, 2023.

2) Read and process *Sacred Rhythms* by Ruth Haley Barton.

3) Read *It's Not Supposed to Be This Way* by Lysa TerKeurst or *Rising Strong* by Brené Brown.

# THE PATHWAY TO PEACE

*Distress and anxiety are weights
too heavy to carry.*

As you read Chapter 7: "The Pathway to Peace" in *Death by Pastoring*, review, reflect on, and respond to the text by answering the following questions.

# REVIEW, REFLECT, AND RESPOND:

In what ways does stress impact the pathway to peace?

_____

_____

_____

_____

_____

_____

_____

_____

_____

_____

_____

_____

_____

_____

_____

_____

_____

_____

_____

_____

_____

_____

_____

What is God's recommended approach to dealing with emotional, spiritual, and mental weights that hinder us?

_____

_____

_____

_____

_____

_____

_____

_____

_____

_____

What is the significance of the Greek word "apotethimi" (cast off or throw away) in the context of throwing off burdens, as explained in this chapter?

_____

_____

_____

_____

_____

_____

_____

_____

_____

_____

_____

How do the world and the devil shape the perception of ministry successes and failures, and what is the truth the text presents in contrast?

_____

_____

_____

_____

_____

_____

_____

_____

_____

_____

_____

What is the purpose of your existence, according to Isaiah 61:3?

_____

_____

_____

_____

_____

_____

_____

_____

_____

_____

_____

_____

In the context of leadership stress, what does Jesus promise to His disciples, and how is this related to the concept of obedience?

_____

_____

_____

_____

_____

_____

_____

_____

_____

_____

_____

> *Dear friends, now we are children of God, and what we will be has not yet been made known. But we know that when Christ appears, we shall be like him, for we shall see him as he is. All who have this hope in him purify themselves, just as he is pure.*
>
> **—1 John 3:2-3**

*Consider the scripture above and answer the following question:*

How does this passage bring you peace?

_____

_____

_____

_____

_____

_____

# HEALTHY HEARTBEATS FOR
## The Pathway to Peace

1) Read *The Ruthless Elimination of Hurry* by John Mark Comer and *Subversive Sabbath* by A. J. Swoboda.

2) Read and process *Emotionally Healthy Spirituality* by Peter Scazzero.

3) Look over the "Tracing Behavior Back to Belief" in the Resources. Follow the examples and plug in a behavior or emotion you commonly have; trace it back to a core heart belief.

# LEADING IN A YOKE

*The symbolism is clear. Jesus commands us to attach ourselves to him. To work with him. Only him, forever.*

## READING TIME

As you read Chapter 8: "Leading in a Yoke" in *Death by Pastoring*, review, reflect on, and respond to the text by answering the following questions.

# REVIEW, REFLECT, AND RESPOND:

How does Jesus use the analogy of oxen yoked together to explain the connection between work and soul rest?

_____

_____

_____

_____

_____

_____

_____

_____

_____

What is the significance of the staple in the yoke that encircles the heads of two oxen, horses, or mules?

_____

_____

_____

_____

_____

_____

_____

_____

_____

_____

_____

In what ways does the partnership of two yoked oxen demonstrate the principle of multiplied power, and how does this relate to working with Jesus?

_____

_____

_____

_____

_____

_____

_____

_____

_____

_____

How are yoked oxen trained, and why is it essential for them to work together, learning each other's moves?

_____

_____

_____

_____

_____

_____

_____

_____

_____

_____

_____

_____

According to this chapter, why is Jesus' work considered easy, and how does working with Him make our work easy?

_____

_____

_____

_____

_____

_____

_____

_____

_____

_____

In what manner does perfectionism impact an individual's calling, and what are some signs that someone might be struggling with perfectionism?

_____

_____

_____

_____

_____

_____

_____

_____

_____

_____

> *Take my yoke upon you and learn from me, for I am gentle and humble in heart, and you will find rest for your souls.*
>
> —Matthew 11:29

*Consider the scripture above and answer the following questions:*

What does it mean to take Jesus's yoke?

_____

_____

_____

_____

_____

_____

_____

_____

What does rest for the soul look and feel like? Have you experienced this?

_____

_____

_____

_____

_____

_____

_____

_____

_____

# HEALTHY HEARTBEATS FOR
## Leading in a Yoke

1) Read *The 21 Irrefutable Laws of Leadership* by John Maxwell and *Dare to Lead* by Brené Brown.

2) Take the "Avoidance Assessment" in the Resources at the back of the book.

3) List situations or feelings that make you spiral into discouragement, avoidance, or despair; find the lie embedded in them and pray against it.

_____

_____

_____

_____

_____

_____

_____

4) Identify a person in ministry who frustrates or irritates you. Commit to praying for that person. Look for opportunities to help this person develop their strengths.

_____

_____

_____

_____

_____

_____

_____

# STEWARDS AND OWNERS

*Stewardship is not simply taking care of something, like house-sitting or babysitting, although those actions require careful attention and responsibility. Stewardship demands investment and multiplication.*

## READING TIME

As you read Chapter 9: "Stewards and Owners" in *Death by Pastoring*, review, reflect on, and respond to the text by answering the following questions.

# REVIEW, REFLECT, AND RESPOND:

What is the difference between ownership and stewardship? Do you own the ministry, or are you a steward of it?

_____

_____

_____

_____

_____

_____

_____

_____

_____

_____

_____

_____

_____

_____

_____

_____

_____

_____

_____

_____

_____

_____

_____

_____

What happens when individuals attempt ownership of the ministries they manage for God, and why is it stressed that the weight of the ministry is not meant to be owned?

_____

_____

_____

_____

_____

_____

_____

_____

_____

_____

What insights does the Parable of the Talents (Matthew 25:14-30) provide regarding stewardship and the relationship between the master and the servants?

_____

_____

_____

_____

_____

_____

_____

_____

_____

_____

In what ways can pastors and leaders fall into the trap of comparing themselves with others, and how does this comparison contribute to stress and insecurity?

_____

_____

_____

_____

_____

_____

_____

_____

_____

_____

_____

This chapter mentions the importance of stewarding peace. What are the five words suggested to guide individuals in stewarding a peaceful work ethic, and how are they applicable in a ministry context?

_____

_____

_____

_____

_____

_____

_____

_____

_____

_____

What are the consequences for the servant who failed to invest the talent in the Parable of the Talents, and how does this relate to the concept that the gifts entrusted to individuals are not meant for personal use but stewardship?

_____

_____

_____

_____

_____

_____

_____

_____

_____

*But the one who does not know and does things deserving punishment will be beaten with few blows. From everyone who has been given much, much will be demanded; and from the one who has been entrusted with much, much more will be asked.*

**— Luke 12:48 (NIV)**

*Consider the scripture above and answer the following question:*

What does this verse reveal about our expected stewardship?

_____

_____

_____

_____

_____

# HEALTHY HEARTBEATS FOR
## Stewards and Owners

1) Analyze your stress-inducing responsibilities. Is it possible that you've taken ownership of your success? Put your responsibilities on the altar; give control back to God.

_____

_____

_____

_____

2) 'Which of your responsibilities or stressors can you entrust someone else to manage for you? Choose to give others the freedom to steward an area for God's approval, not yours.

_____

_____

_____

_____

_____

3) Watch Dave Ramsey's conference session "Leading with Stewardship" on YouTube (or any of his stewardship talks).

4) Look at the 4 Fs to determine where you can grow in your stewardship: faith, family, finances, and fitness. How are you stewarding your spiritual growth, your family, your money, and your health? What needs to change?

_____

_____

_____

_____

5) Read *Strengthening the Soul of Your Leadership* by Ruth Haley Barton.

# CHAPTER 10

# A LIGHTER LOAD

*Work is all about God. It's never about us.*

## REVIEW, REFLECT, AND RESPOND:

How does Jesus' relationship with His Father work as an example to emphasize the concept of stewardship in our work?

_____

_____

_____

_____

_____

_____

_____

_____

_____

_____

_____

_____

_____

_____

_____

_____

_____

_____

_____

_____

_____

_____

_____

According to this chapter, what is the curse on mankind in relation to work, and how does it differ from the blessing of work that God originally intended?

_____

_____

_____

_____

_____

_____

_____

_____

_____

_____

How can one's work effectively point people to God, and what role does belief play in achieving this? Does your work effectively accomplish this?

_____

_____

_____

_____

_____

_____

_____

_____

_____

_____

In discussing the concept of "greater works" (John 14:12), what examples from the history of the church does this chapter mention, and how does the Holy Spirit play a role in enabling believers to accomplish greater things?

_____

_____

_____

_____

_____

_____

_____

_____

_____

_____

How can individuals maintain peace and avoid distress in the face of adversity, according to this chapter?

_____

_____

_____

_____

_____

_____

_____

_____

_____

_____

_____

> *Believe me when I say that I am in the Father and the Father is in me; or at least believe on the evidence of the works themselves. Very truly I tell you, whoever believes in me will do the works I have been doing, and they will do even greater things than these, because I am going to the Father. And I will do whatever you ask in my name, so that the Father may be glorified in the Son.*
>
> —John 14:11-13 (NIV)

*Consider the scripture above and answer the following questions:*

How does this passage help lighten your load?

_____

_____

_____

_____

_____

_____

_____

What is the meaning of these scriptures?

_____

_____

_____

_____

_____

_____

_____

_____

# HEALTHY HEARTBEATS FOR
## A Lighter Load

1) What would make your work lighter? What tasks do you need to offload?

_____

_____

_____

_____

_____

_____

2) Ask your spouse or a key leader to help you identify areas where you could lighten your load and steward your time and talents more effectively.

3) Read *Addicted to Busy: Recovery for the Rushed Soul* by Brady Boyd and *The Emotionally Healthy Church* by Peter Scazzero.

4) Identify one task you guard from anyone's interference. Consider the idolatrous implications of this obsession. Confess it and give it to God completely.

# PART THREE

# A NEW WAY TO REST (THE REDEMPTION OF STRESS)

# THE GOOD SHEPHERD

*Rest and water are life, and the
shepherd finds them for his sheep.*

## READING TIME

As you read Chapter 11: "The Good Shepherd" in *Death by Pastoring*, review, reflect on, and respond to the text by answering the following questions.

# REVIEW, REFLECT, AND RESPOND:

What are some reasons that shepherding is considered one of the least stressful jobs, and how do these insights relate to handling stress in the context of Psalm 23?

_____

_____

_____

_____

_____

_____

_____

_____

_____

_____

_____

_____

_____

_____

_____

_____

_____

_____

_____

_____

_____

_____

This chapter draws parallels between farm life and the Christian life, mentioning that, "Scripture calls us sheep." In what ways does the nature of sheep mirror the characteristics and needs of believers?

_____

_____

_____

_____

_____

_____

_____

_____

_____

What are the lessons from, and how do they emphasize the relational aspect of the shepherd-sheep analogy?

_____

_____

_____

_____

_____

_____

_____

_____

_____

_____

How does the text describe the role of a shepherd in guiding and protecting sheep, and what qualities of a good shepherd are highlighted in the analogies provided?

_____

_____

_____

_____

_____

_____

_____

_____

_____

This chapter emphasizes the importance of pastors and ministry leaders behaving like sheep despite their role as spiritual shepherds. What paradigm shift does Jesus require, and how does this impact the leadership style of pastors and ministry leaders?

_____

_____

_____

_____

_____

_____

_____

_____

_____

_____

> *The LORD is my shepherd, I lack nothing. He makes me lie down in green pastures, he leads me beside quiet waters. . . .*
>
> —Psalm 23:1-2 (NIV)

*Consider the scripture above and answer the following question:*

In what ways is God comparable to a shepherd?

_____

_____

_____

_____

_____

_____

_____

_____

_____

_____

# HEALTHY HEARTBEATS FOR
## The Good Shepherd

1) Quantify contentment. You've heard of counting your blessings. Get specific and enumerate where you find contentment in the Lord. Do it daily. List how your Shepherd provides for you.

_____

_____

_____

_____

_____

_____

_____

_____

2) Spend time with your Shepherd. Bring him your stress and leave with his rest.

3) Read *How Happiness Happens: Finding Lasting Joy in a World of Comparison, Disappointment, and Unmet Expectations* by Max Lucado or *Faith Meets Therapy* by Anthony Evans and Stacy Kaiser, MA, LMFT.

4) Establish regular times for your staff and family to testify of God's blessings, to notice where He's working, and to celebrate His work.

# REST VERSUS RESTORATION

*Rest is preventative. Restoration is curative. Jesus rested; he did not push himself to the point of crashing.*

As you read
Chapter 12:
"Rest Versus
Restoration"
in *Death by
Pastoring*,
review, reflect
on, and respond
to the text by
answering
the following
questions.

# REVIEW, REFLECT, AND RESPOND:

What role does being yoked to Jesus play in preventing burnout?

_____

_____

_____

_____

_____

_____

_____

_____

_____

_____

_____

_____

_____

_____

_____

_____

_____

_____

_____

_____

_____

_____

_____

_____

In Psalm 23:3, the phrase "He restoreth my soul" (KJV) is discussed in the context of restoration. How does the text elaborate on the concept of restoration, and what distinguishes it from mere rest?

_____

_____

_____

_____

_____

_____

_____

_____

_____

_____

The author emphasizes the importance of seeking restoration in desolate places and embracing an insatiable thirst for the Lord. How does the text explain the significance of thirst in driving individuals to seek the Lord, especially in challenging circumstances?

_____

_____

_____

_____

_____

_____

_____

_____

_____

_____

_____

In your own words, what are the differences between rest and restoration?

_____

_____

_____

_____

_____

_____

_____

_____

_____

_____

Psalm 24:3-5 outlines the requirements for intimacy with God, focusing on clean hands, a pure heart, and the absence of trust in idols. How do these requirements relate to the process of restoration, and why is worship a key element in this process?

_____

_____

_____

_____

_____

_____

_____

_____

_____

_____

> *. . . he refreshes my soul. He guides me along the right paths for his name's sake.*
>
> —Psalm 23:3 (NIV)

*Consider the scripture above and answer the following question:*

What does it mean when God guides us along the right paths "for his name's sake"?

_____

_____

_____

_____

_____

_____

_____

_____

_____

_____

_____

_____

# HEALTHY HEARTBEATS FOR
## Rest Versus Restoration

1) Read *Restoring Balance to Your Life* by Dr. Richard Swenson and *Leading on Empty: Refilling Your Tank and Renewing Your Passion* by Wayne Cordeiro.

2) Take out your calendar and block off time for restoration: 1 hour/day, 1 day/week, 1 weekend/month, 1 month/year. Plan spiritual retreats, family vacations, and dates (and vacations) with your spouse. Plan rest days on your vacation.

3) Consider blocking off your day into thirds: 8 hours sleep, 8 hours work, 8 hours family and fun.

4) Choose a conduit for restoration (it must be relaxing, not something on your to-do list). Consider:

❏ Silence
❏ Changes to evening, bed, and waking routines
❏ Exercise
❏ Art
❏ Romancing your spouse
❏ Yardwork
❏ Reading
❏ A restful location
❏ Music
❏ Building, tinkering, or fixing things
❏ Diet of healthy food—cut out everything with preservatives
❏ A mission trip that you're not leading

# NEW WALK, SAME VALLEY

*Grief persists until you fully deal with it.*

As you read
Chapter 13:
"New Walk,
Same Valley"
in *Death by
Pastoring*,
review, reflect
on, and respond
to the text by
answering
the following
questions.

# REVIEW, REFLECT, AND RESPOND:

How did Sue's early memories shape her perception of grief and loss, especially considering her father's death in a plane crash when she was just two years old? How have your memories shaped your perception of grief and loss?

_____

_____

_____

_____

_____

_____

_____

_____

_____

_____

_____

_____

_____

_____

_____

_____

_____

_____

_____

_____

_____

Think about how Sue's family coped with the loss of her father, given the limited resources for dealing with grief and trauma in the late 1960s. Have you ever responded to grief in a similar way? Describe the experience.

_____

_____

_____

_____

_____

_____

_____

_____

_____

What role does the concept of an "orphan spirit" play in Sue's understanding of grief and its potential impact on leaders, particularly those who lead alone? Have you ever experienced this harmful spirit? What was the result?

_____

_____

_____

_____

_____

_____

_____

_____

_____

_____

What are the symbolic meanings of the rod and staff mentioned in Psalm 23:4, and how do they relate to God's role in comforting and guiding individuals through challenging times?

_____

_____

_____

_____

_____

_____

_____

_____

_____

_____

How important are community and vulnerability among pastors? In what ways can isolation be the devil's strongest move against spiritual leaders?

_____

_____

_____

_____

_____

_____

_____

_____

_____

_____

> *This is the message we have heard from him and declare to you: God is light; in him there is no darkness at all. If we claim to have fellowship with him and yet walk in the darkness, we lie and do not live out the truth. But if we walk in the light, as he is in the light, we have fellowship with one another, and the blood of Jesus, his Son, purifies us from all sin.*
>
> —1 John 1:5-7 (NIV)

*Consider the scripture above and answer the following questions:*

What does it mean to "walk in the light"?

_____

_____

_____

_____

_____

_____

_____

_____

What stands out to you from this passage of scripture?

_____

_____

_____

_____

_____

_____

_____

# HEALTHY HEARTBEATS FOR
## New Walk, Same Valley

1) Take the "Fight Fear Assessment" in the Resources. This chart can help you identify your fears and replace the embedded lies with the truth of Scripture.

2) Read *Father Hunger* by Robert S. McGee.

3) Share the gospel with someone; spend time with new believers. Nothing corrects your perspective on life better than seekers and new believers.

4) Get a professional grief counselor or grief therapist; go regularly.

5) Reach across denominational lines and invite pastors (and their spouses) to get coffee or lunch with you. Find out how they're doing. Share, empathize, encourage. Become friends.

# A SEAT AT THE TABLE

*The dinner table means family. It shows everyone that they belong, that they're important enough for someone to do the work to satisfy their cravings.*

As you read Chapter 14: "A Seat at the Table" in *Death by Pastoring*, review, reflect on, and respond to the text by answering the following questions.

# REVIEW, REFLECT, AND RESPOND:

How does the fear of brokenness affect our tendency to hide our failures and struggles?

_____

_____

_____

_____

_____

_____

_____

_____

_____

_____

_____

_____

_____

_____

_____

_____

_____

_____

_____

_____

_____

_____

_____

Why do people hide their brokenness out of shame and pride? Have you ever done this?

_____

_____

_____

_____

_____

_____

_____

_____

_____

_____

What does the family table symbolize, and why is it considered a special place?

_____

_____

_____

_____

_____

_____

_____

_____

_____

_____

_____

_____

In what ways does the imagery of God preparing a table for us relate to the family table mentioned?

_____

_____

_____

_____

_____

_____

_____

_____

_____

_____

Why does the author believe that enemies, as described in Psalm 23:5, are not necessarily individuals who physically endanger us, but rather those who disagree with our ideas or perspectives?

_____

_____

_____

_____

_____

_____

_____

_____

_____

_____

> *You prepare a table before me in the presence of my enemies. You anoint my head with oil; my cup overflows.*
>
> **—Psalm 23:5 (NIV)**

*Consider the scripture above and answer the following questions:*

What is the significance of sitting at a table prepared in the presence of your enemies?

_____

_____

_____

_____

_____

_____

_____

_____

What does the overflowing cup represent in this passage?

_____

_____

_____

_____

_____

_____

_____

_____

_____

# ACTION STEPS FOR
## A Seat at the Table

1) Read *Don't Give Your Enemy a Seat at the Table* by Louie Giglio.

2) Prioritize table time with family and friends. Practice affirming and listening. Talk about "highs" and "lows" from the day. Lay hands and pray over one another.

3) Analyze your "table time" at work. Make sure your staff feels safe at the table, desk, or conference room with you. Ask them how you can improve meetings to make everyone comfortable with vulnerability, suggestions, and critique. Covenant together to be honest and kind in your disagreements.

4) When you disagree with your spouse or a colleague, fight fair. Lay the ground rules. Create a safe environment. Listen carefully. Make sure you understand. Affirm your love for them.

# IN MY FATHER'S HOUSE

*Don't quit your calling.*

## READING TIME

As you read
Chapter 15:
"In My Father's
House" in *Death
by Pastoring*,
review, reflect
on, and respond
to the text by
answering
the following
questions.

# REVIEW, REFLECT, AND RESPOND:

What is the difference between staying in your
current ministry and staying in your calling?

_____

_____

_____

_____

_____

_____

_____

_____

_____

_____

_____

_____

_____

_____

_____

_____

_____

_____

_____

_____

_____

_____

_____

_____

How does this chapter define and explain the meanings of the Hebrew words "tob" (goodness) and "hesed" (mercy) in the context of Psalm 23:6?

_____

_____

_____

_____

_____

_____

_____

_____

_____

In the discussion of Jesus' last words to His disciples, what promises does Jesus make about preparing a home for His followers, and how can leaders be encouraged by this to trust in God's preparation for them?

_____

_____

_____

_____

_____

_____

_____

_____

_____

_____

What practical suggestions does this chapter provide for leaders to stay in the will of God?

_____

_____

_____

_____

_____

_____

_____

_____

_____

What are the dangers of nurturing and excusing stress in leadership? What does this chapter suggest about the true calling and destiny fulfilled by Jesus on the cross?

_____

_____

_____

_____

_____

_____

_____

_____

_____

_____

> *Blessed are the merciful, for they will be shown mercy.*
>
> —Matthew 5:7 (NIV)

*Consider the scripture above and answer the following question:*

In what ways can you demonstrate mercy in your life?

_____

_____

_____

_____

_____

_____

_____

_____

_____

_____

_____

# HEALTHY HEARTBEATS FOR
## In My Father's House

1) Identify your growth team—counselor, coaches, mentors, prayer warriors, and friends.

2) Take the stress test and regularly examine your physical, emotional, mental, and, of course, spiritual well-being. But please don't stop with the spiritual. You are not a healthy leader if you only care for your soul.

3) Identify self-care, soul-care, and growth habits and rhythms. Keep working at it until you get a good rhythm.

4) Plan your sabbath.

5) Find resources. Subscribe to *Stress Test Podcast* by texting "stress" to 833-204-2158.

Interact with us via email, Facebook, or Instagram.

www.ingramcontent.com/pod-product-compliance
Lightning Source LLC
Chambersburg PA
CBHW062118080426
42734CB00012B/2904